Look with us at
ANIMALS

by Karen O'Callaghan

Illustrated by

E. Rowe, R. Morton and T. Hayward

Brimax Books·Newmarket·England

ISBN 0 86112 190 2
© Brimax Rights Ltd. 1983
Published by Brimax Books
Newmarket England 1983
Fourth printing 1985.
Printed in Belgium

Buying a pet

Our puppy needs...

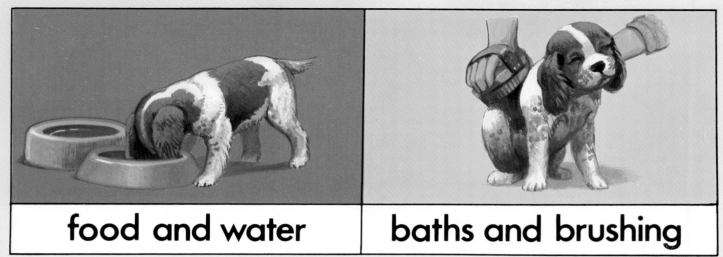

food and water

baths and brushing

walks and play

plenty of sleep

and lots of love.

cat

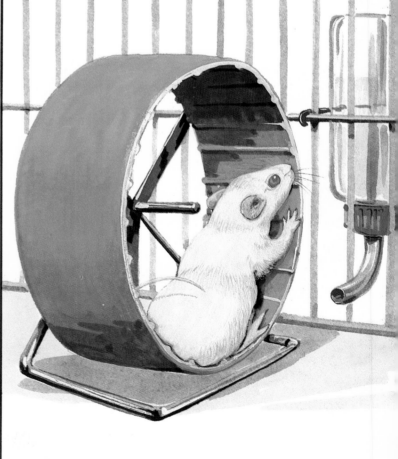

rabbit

goldfish

mouse

guinea pig

tortoise

budgerigar

hamster

In the garden

spider and web

earwigs

butterfly

snails

ladybirds

sparrow

woodlice

worms

ants

caterpillars

On the seashore

seagulls

limpets

hermit crabs

crabs

sea urchins

anemones

periwinkles

whelks

starfish

mussels

On the farm

cow

donkey

horse

dog

sheep

chickens

Families and babies

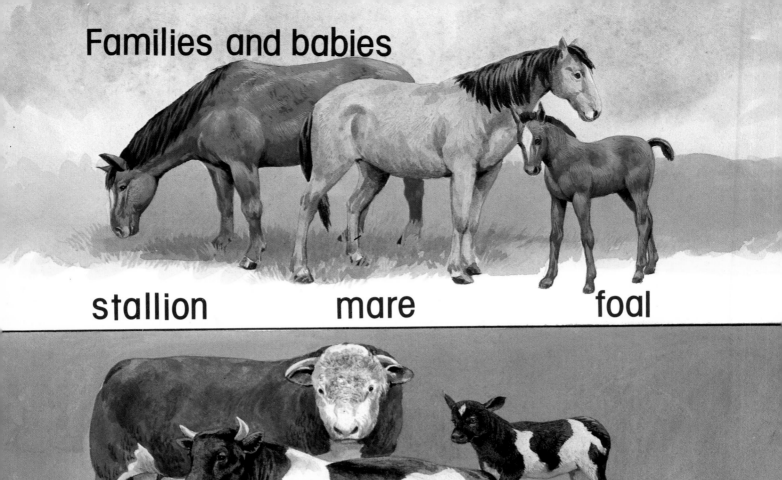

stallion   mare   foal

bull   cow   calf

billy-goat   nanny-goat   kid

cockerel   hen   chick

boar   sow   piglet

ram   ewe   lamb

drake   duck   duckling

buck   doe   fawn

lion   lioness   cub

Some animals with pouches

sugar
glider

koala

opossum

kangaroo

wombat

Tasmanian devil

hen

cat

horse

donkey

sheep

cow

pig goat duck

"My animals live with people.
They are tame."

elephant

zebra

tiger

lion

buffalo

polar bear

fox   kangaroo   stoat

"My animals live free all over
the world. They are wild."

puma – mountain lion –cougar

lynx

jaguar

leopard

lion

The tiger's stripes hide him in the long grass.
He likes to swim but never climbs trees.

The cheetah has long legs. He can run faster
than any other animal.

In the hot grassland

buffalo

zebra

stork

Grant's gazelle

giraffe

ostrich

rhinoceros

warthog

hyena

The elephants are cool in the water. They squirt water with their trunks.

The giraffe curls its long tongue round the leaves at the top of the tree.

Mother <u>crocodile</u> is gentle as she takes her babies into the water.

The baby <u>hippopotamus</u> is born under the water. He loves to be wet and muddy.

The <u>anteater</u> licks up the ants. He cannot open his mouth and he has no teeth.

The <u>flamingoes</u> feed with their heads upsidedown and their bills in the water.

These <u>camels</u> have two humps and long shaggy hair.
They live in the desert.

The <u>Gila-monster</u> is a poisonous lizard. He moves
slowly in the hot sun.

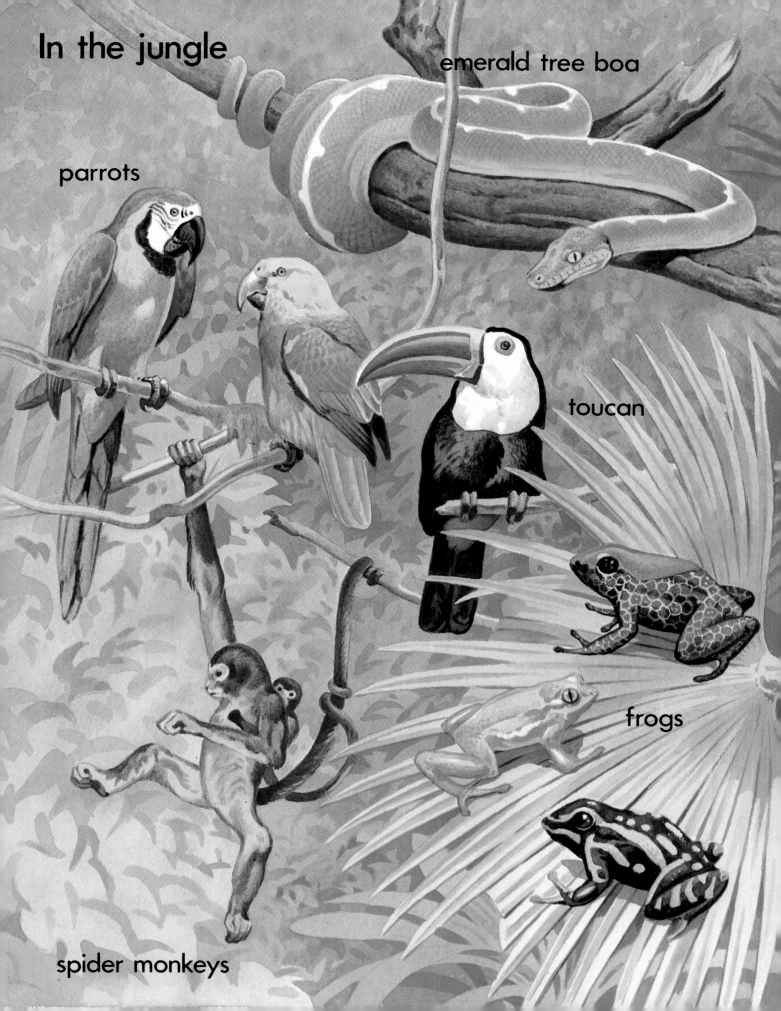

In the jungle

emerald tree boa

parrots

toucan

frogs

spider monkeys

The orang-utan walks slowly along the branches. He
does not swing or jump.

The gorillas are big and strong. They are also quiet
and gentle.

The chimpanzee has a drink. He does not play in the water and cannot swim.

The chameleon lives in trees. He uses his long sticky tongue to catch food.

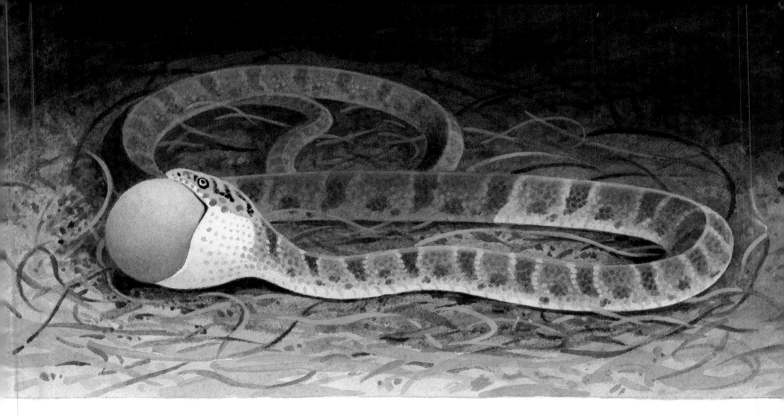

This egg-eating <u>snake</u> has no teeth. He swallows the egg and spits out the shell.

The giant <u>panda</u> eats bamboo. He lives in the forest high in the mountains.

In the cold lands

musk oxen

grey wolves

arctic fox

arctic hare

reindeer

seals

Mother polar bear keeps her cubs warm in their
den under the snow.

The walrus uses its tusks to climb out of the
water and up the ice.

The sea-lions use their flippers to swim
and to move on the ice.

Father penguin keeps the baby chick warm.
Mother hunts in the water for food.

In a storm the mother <u>yaks</u> will make a circle round their babies to keep them warm.

In the winter the <u>moose</u> digs away the snow with his hooves to find food.

The big-horn sheep have thick woolly coats
to keep them warm in the winter.

The golden eagle carries sticks back to its
nest high in the mountains.

In the woods

grey squirrel

owl

red squirrel

fox

weasel

stoat

hedgehog

The <u>badgers</u> live under the ground. At night they come out to look for food.

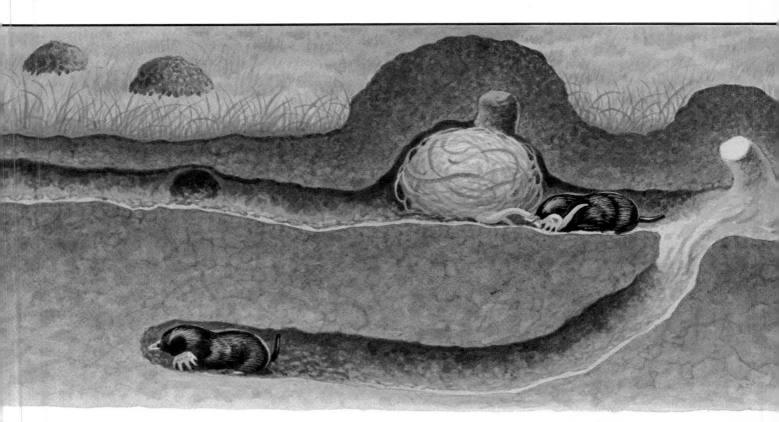

The <u>moles</u> dig tunnels with their front paws. They are looking for worms.

In the forest

brown bear

porcupine

racoon

rattlesnake

skunk

chipmunk

The otter's long whiskers help him to feel his way through the muddy water.

The beaver uses his strong teeth to chop down the trees to make his home.

The prairie dog is on guard. He will warn the others if there is danger.

The black bear cubs stay up in the tree when mother bear goes hunting.

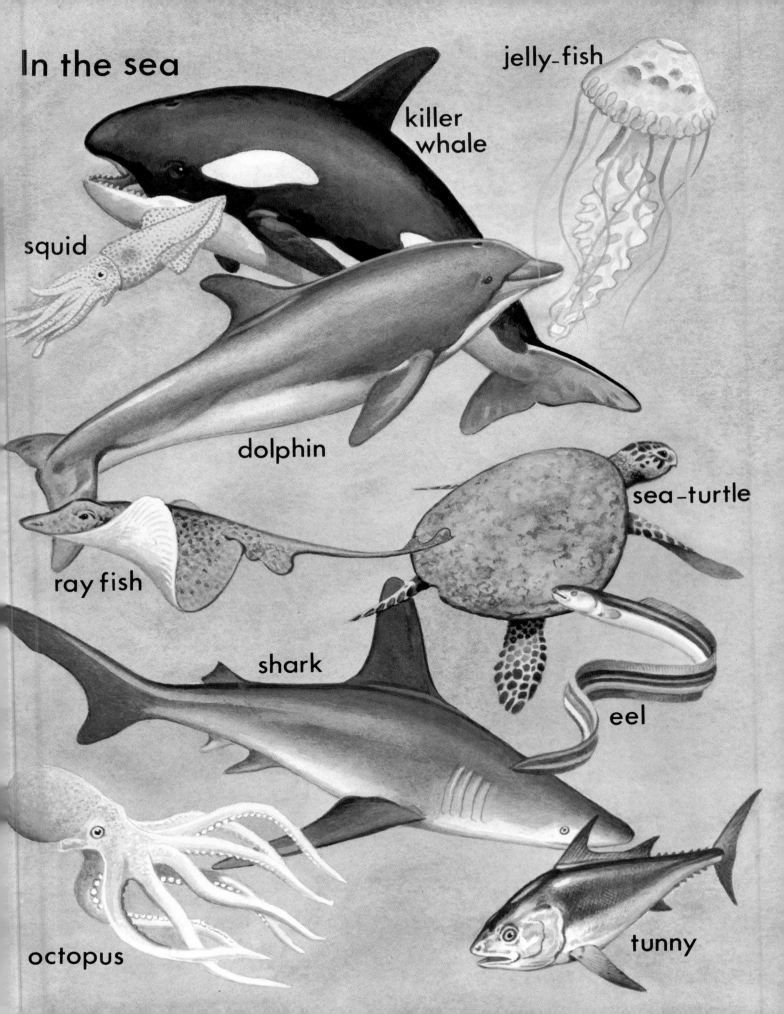

In the sea

killer whale

jelly-fish

squid

dolphin

ray fish

sea-turtle

shark

eel

octopus

tunny

Do you know?

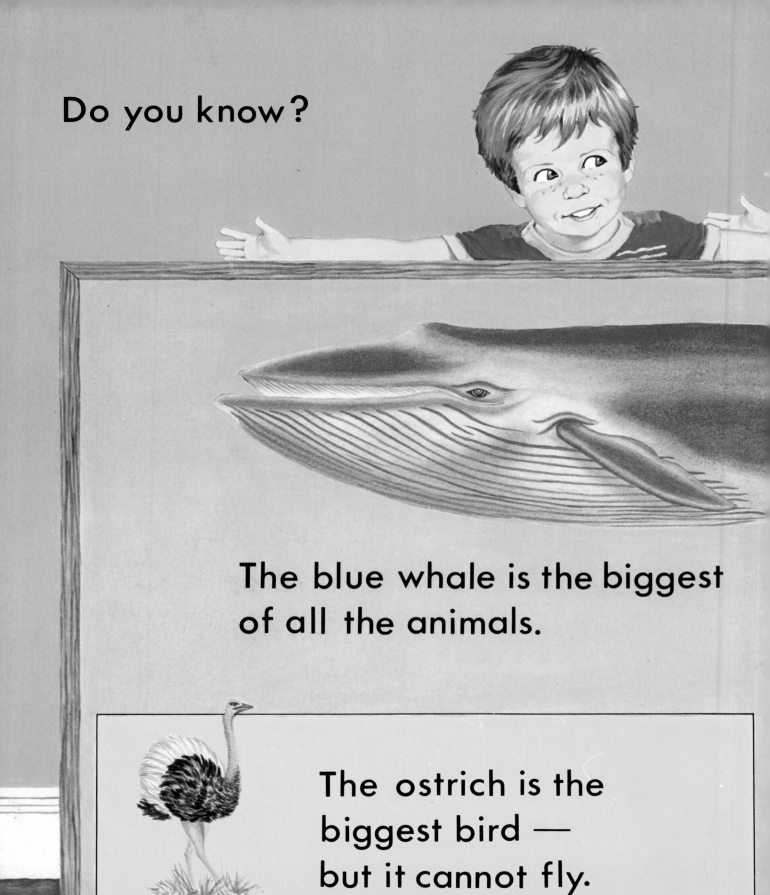

The blue whale is the biggest
of all the animals.

The ostrich is the
biggest bird —
but it cannot fly.

The biggest
animal on land
is the elephant.

A giraffe
sleeps standing up.